Awestruck

A YEARLONG JOURNAL

52 Experiments to Find
Wonder, Joy, and Meaning
in Everyday Life

Alexandra Franzen

CHRONICLE BOOKS
SAN FRANCISCO

ISBN 978-1-7972-2759-7

Manufactured in China.

Design by Wynne Au-Yeung.

10 9 8 7 6 5 4 3 2 1

Chronicle Books publishes distinctive books and gifts. From
award-winning children's titles, bestselling cookbooks, and
eclectic pop culture to acclaimed works of art and design,
stationery, and journals, we craft publishing that's instantly
recognizable for its spirit and creativity. Enjoy our publishing and
become part of our community at www.chroniclebooks.com.

Special quantity discounts are available to corporations and
other organizations. Contact our premiums department at
corporatesales@chroniclebooks.com or at 1-800-759-0190.

Chronicle Books LLC
680 Second Street
San Francisco, California 94107
www.chroniclebooks.com

Introduction

WHAT IS AWE?

Some describe awe as an overwhelming feeling of wonder, magic, and mystery.

The way you feel when you witness a sunrise,
eclipse, or shooting star.

Some say it's excitement tinged with humility, respect, or even fear.

The way you feel when you see lightning shattering
the sky or hear the booming sound of thunder.

For many, it's a feeling of reverence—feeling small in the presence of something big and mighty.

The way you feel when you stand at the base of
a redwood tree that's towering above you.

Awe can come from feeling a baby curl their tiny hand around your finger, looking at a glittering city skyline, soaring above the clouds in an airplane, or listening to an exquisite piece of music.

However you define awe, you know it when you feel it.

THE SCIENCE OF AWE

What is awe according to science? Does it happen randomly? Or are there specific things we can do to spark this emotion?

Two researchers, Dacher Keltner and Jonathan Haidt, came together to explore the big question "what causes awe?" They reported their findings in a paper titled "Approaching Awe." I'll save you the trouble of reading the entire paper—although it's very interesting and worth a look if you're curious. The researchers present the idea that you need *two ingredients* to feel awe.

One: an experience that challenges your "current mental structures."

This means an experience that's different from your typical routine. It's new and fresh. It interrupts a predictable pattern. It doesn't fit what you expected. It might challenge something you used to believe and cause you to see the world from a new perspective. It sparks that feeling of "whoa . . . this is different."

This doesn't necessarily mean doing something completely new, like skydiving. It can mean doing something ordinary, like taking a walk, but doing it in a new way. It's any experience that gives you a jolt of newness and novelty.

Two: "perceived vastness."

You sense that you're in the presence of something vast. Something bigger and greater than yourself. This could be something physically big, like the Grand Canyon. Or something emotionally big, like witnessing an astounding moment of courage or an exquisitely beautiful piece of art that takes your breath away.

When these two things—*novelty* and *vastness*—are experienced at once, it activates your brain in a particular way and generates the emotion we call *awe*.

Intuitively, this makes sense. For instance, many people feel awe when they see a shooting star. That's because it's special and different, not necessarily something you see every night (*novelty*) and reminds you how tiny you are in the big scheme of things (*vastness*).

AWE IN YOUR LIFE

Can you remember a time when you felt awe—even just for a few seconds?

Were you standing at the peak of a mountain? Watching a jaw-dropping performance? Witnessing the power of the human spirit—through breathtaking love, forgiveness, or bravery?

In that moment, you were experiencing novelty and vastness—the magic combination that sparks awe. You have felt it before. You can feel it again. You can experience awe every day, if you choose to.

When I think about my strongest moments of awe, two memories come to mind: watching a humpback whale leaping from the ocean, and seeing my daughter, Nora, wiggling her little fingers on the ultrasound screen during my twenty-week prenatal checkup. Both moments were different from my typical routine (*novelty*). And in both moments, I felt humbled in the presence of powers so big and mysterious (*vastness*).

Awe is very personal. What sparks awe for one person may not produce awe for another. If you've never visited the ocean before, seeing a whale might leave you overwhelmed with awe. On the other hand, if you're a third-generation boat captain and you've spent your entire life on the sea, seeing a whale might not do it for you.

AWE IN YOUR BODY

What does awe physically feel like in your body? How can you recognize when you're experiencing a moment of awe?

Many people report feeling physical sensations or reactions when they feel awestruck. They say things like:

"I felt goosebumps."

"My jaw dropped."

"It took my breath away."

"My eyes welled up with tears."

"I felt shivers down my spine."

"My heart expanded."

"I got choked up."

Awe manifests in a variety of ways. The way one person experiences awe may be different from the sensations that you feel.

AWE IN YOUR BRAIN

Not only does awe manifest in your body through physical sensations, such as shivers and tears, but it also affects your brain in fascinating ways.

Andrew Newberg is a neuroscientist who studies transcendent experiences like meditation and prayer. Says Newberg, when you experience awe, your brain's parietal lobe temporarily shuts down.

The parietal lobe controls proprioception (your ability to spatially determine where your body is) and helps you create a visual map of the world around you. This lobe helps tell you, "I am over here. That tree is over there. That person is over there," so you can distinguish between different points.

When there's decreased activity in the parietal lobe, what happens? "A loss of the boundary between the self and other things in the world, and ultimately a sense of oneness and connectedness," says Newberg.

Because awe reduces activity in the parietal lobe, it blurs the boundary between "you" and "everything else." This is why when you're experiencing awe, you feel less individualistic and more connected to everything around you. You may feel connected to nature, to people, to the universe, or to God, whatever God means to you.

Dacher Keltner, one of the world's top researchers on awe, describes this as the shift from the "isolated self" to the "integrated self."

The science of awe is a very new field. According to Keltner, there's still so much we don't understand. But one thing is certain and undeniable: when you experience a little dose of awe, it improves your life immediately.

WHY IS AWE IMPORTANT?

Research shows that awe has myriad benefits and is a crucial component of a healthy, long life.

Awe helps our bodies fight diseases.

One study found that people who feel awe on a regular basis tend to have fewer pro-inflammatory cytokines, the molecules that promote inflammation. We all need a certain amount of these cytokines, but too much isn't a good thing. People with excessively high levels of pro-inflammatory cytokines are more likely to develop diabetes, heart disease, arthritis, and mental health illnesses like depression. A regular dose of awe seems to help keep these cytokines at a healthy level.

Awe reduces stress.

Researchers took military veterans on a white-water rafting trip. The goal: expose people with post-traumatic stress disorder (PTSD) to the awe-inducing power of nature. After the trip, participants had fewer stress-related symptoms and a greater sense of well-being.

Awe improves academic performance.

In a study of four hundred high school students, researchers found that the more awe these students felt, "the more curiosity they expressed and the better they performed in school."

Awe makes us less individualistic.

In another study, participants were shown an awe-inspiring skeleton of a *T. rex*. Then they were asked to describe themselves. These people were more likely to describe themselves as "an inhabitant of the Earth" or "a person" (phrases that convey being part of a larger collective) rather than individualistic phrases like "doctor" or "CEO." Awe shifts our perception from "me" to "we."

Awe makes us feel less busy.

Awe bends our sense of time and makes us feel time-abundant rather than time-poor. After experiencing awe, participants in one study were more likely to agree with statements describing time as plentiful and expansive.

Awe makes us feel less lonely.

Researchers asked fifty-two people to take a fifteen-minute "awe walk" once a week. They were asked to simply notice the world around them, such as the colors of the autumn foliage or the way the light shimmered on a raindrop. After eight weeks, the awe-walkers felt more connected to others and less lonely—even if they'd been walking alone.

WHAT KILLS AWE?

As we bustle through our busy modern lives, it can feel challenging to experience awe.

Neuropsychologist Paul Pearsall says that many people are "awe-deficient." We are awe-deprived, which leaves us in a state of "quiet despair." But how did we get to this point?

Danny Penman, a meditation teacher and journalist who investigates awe, points to a couple of reasons. According to Penman, the biggest awe-killer is too much predictability and sameness. Bland workplaces. Neighborhoods with identical, cookie-cutter housing. Homogenized communities. He also blames our educational systems, which focus on standardized testing (filling in the right multiple-choice box) rather than curiosity and creativity (exploring big questions that have no answers).

Many researchers point to tech overload as another awe-killer. We spend too much time staring at our digital devices—engaged in trivial, meaningless pursuits—which means there's little space in our lives for awe. As professors Luke Fernandez and Susan J. Matt put it, "Rather than gazing at oceans or mountains, we pose in front of them for selfies."

Do tech devices block us from feeling awe? They can. However, on a more hopeful note, we can use our devices to generate awe too. For instance, you can use your phone to hear a stirring piece of music that brings tears to your eyes, or to see a video of your grandchild's first steps. Devices don't necessarily destroy awe. What matters is how we use them.

WE ALL NEED MORE AWE

As Deborah Farmer Kris writes in the *Washington Post*, "awe might be our most overlooked, undervalued emotion."

We all need more awe.

The good news is that awe can happen in tiny, everyday moments. Awe doesn't necessarily require a meteor shower or redwood tree, and it doesn't have to be time-consuming or costly. You can experience awe while commuting to work, walking the dog, or watching herbs sprout on your windowsill.

Awe is attainable in the day-to-day. We are wired to feel it. We simply have to shift our minds and our behavior the smallest bit in order to access it. Much like flicking on a light switch, it doesn't take much effort to create a dramatic change.

That's why this journal was created—to help you experience awe not just once a decade but as a regular part of your life.

HOW TO USE THIS JOURNAL

Awestruck includes 52 tiny experiments—one for every week in a year. Each one gives you a little dose of awe.

You don't need to begin this journal on January 1. Your personal year of awe can begin any day of the year. Whether it's January 1 or June 12 or December 10, you can start today and use this journal for the next 52 weeks.

You don't need to complete the experiments in order from 1 to 52. Hop around if you want. You could do experiment 1, then 4, then 42, then back to 7, and so on. Go in whatever order you like, just be sure to save experiment 52 for the end of the year.

Most of all, remember: You don't necessarily need to climb to the summit of a mountain to experience awe. Awe is waiting in the small, unassuming corners of life. It's all around us.

A YEAR OF

A

we

Open
Your Eyes

Choose something in your immediate surroundings. A potted plant, loaf of bread, fog gathering in the corner of a mirror, your child mashing bananas with their tiny fingers, anything at all. Look twice. First, look with curiosity—as if you've never seen it before. The second time, look with reverence—as if you'll never see it again.

> TODAY: *Meditate on an everyday object.*
> *Look twice, and look closely.*

With your first look, what do you see? How does it make you feel? When you look a second time, as if you'll never see it again, what do you notice? Do you feel differently? Write a few sentences to describe what you saw and what emotions arose for you.

Be
Small

Stand at the base of an enormous building and look up. Go to the edge of the ocean or another vast expanse. If you'd prefer to stay home, watch a video about something big—the deepest valley, the highest mountain, the largest desert.

TODAY: *Go somewhere where you feel small*
in the midst of something very big.

Write about your experience. Where did you go? How did you feel while you were there? What did you think about?

_____

_____

_____

_____

_____

_____

_____

_____

_____

_____

_____

_____

_____

_____

_____

_____

_____

_____

_____

_____

_____

_____

_____

_____

_____

3

Interrupt a Pattern

During a yoga class, the teacher announced, "We're not doing downward dog today."

I was perplexed. Yoga class with no downward dog? That's like a peanut butter and jelly sandwich with no bread! The teacher explained, "Our theme for today is 'interrupting patterns.' I want you to move in unfamiliar ways and break out of your autopilot routine."

The teacher kept surprising us. We skipped familiar poses and never knew what would come next. Throughout class, I remember thinking, "Well, *this* is different" and "I didn't know my body could do . . . *that*!" It was unforgettable.

> TODAY: *Change up your routine or interrupt a familiar pattern.*

If you normally go a certain way to work, take a different route. If you typically watch TV before bed, listen to music. If you're practicing yoga, do your usual routine from beginning to end, and then from end to beginning in reverse.

What pattern did you interrupt? Did you feel awe, or perhaps surprise, or heightened awareness? Perhaps you didn't feel anything notable and that's okay too. Some experiences may evoke awe for you, and others won't. Write about your experience here.

Join a Cause That's Bigger Than You

When you recognize yourself as a small part of a bigger eco-system, it can spark awe.

TODAY: *Join a cause that's meaningful to you.*

March in a protest. Attend a beach cleanup. Sign a petition that will impact millions of lives. Organize a fundraiser to provide relief to people impacted by war or a natural disaster. By connecting with a greater cause, you'll experience what psychologists call "the small self": the feeling of being part of something bigger than your own individual life.

Write about the cause you chose. Why did you choose this cause? What did you do? How did it make you feel?

Listen to Music That Sparks Awe

Music has an immediate impact on your brain. Professors Kiminobu Sugaya, a neuroscientist, and Ayako Yonetani, a world-renowned violinist, note that music can evoke memories, affect your ability to perceive time, and even help repair damage to the brain.

TODAY: *Listen to a piece of music that touches your heart.*

If there's a particular song you love that always stirs deep emotion, listen to that. Alternatively, go exploring online or visit your local record store and find a song you've never heard before.

What piece of music did you listen to? How did it make you feel?
EXTRA CREDIT: *If you were building a personal playlist of Ten Songs to Spark Awe, what would you put on it?*

_____

_____

_____

_____

_____

_____

_____

_____

_____

_____

_____

_____

_____

_____

_____

_____

_____

_____

_____

_____

_____

Give Thanks for a Miracle

My friend Robert had the opportunity of a lifetime—to produce and host his own TV show. This show would provide inspiration to millions and change lives for the better. However, he needed to raise a significant amount of money to start filming.

With less than twenty-four hours before the deadline, and still a bit short on cash, Robert did something brave. He contacted a wealthy CEO and asked for five minutes of this man's time.

Despite feeling incredibly nervous, Robert sat across from the CEO, told his story, and asked for an investment of $150,000.

The next morning, the CEO said "I believe in your project and want to help. I'm in." He wired the funds.

Robert asked for a miracle, and he got it.

Think about a time in your own life when a miracle happened. You got funding in the nick of time. A friend came to your aid. You missed a flight and then met your future spouse in the airport lounge.

> TODAY: *Take a moment to give thanks for this miracle. Be awed by how wondrous and mysterious life can be.*

Write about your own miracle. What happened? Why are you grateful for it?

_____

_____

_____

_____

_____

_____

_____

_____

_____

_____

_____

_____

_____

_____

_____

_____

_____

_____

_____

_____

_____

Take an
Awe Walk

Your next experiment is simple yet powerful.

> TODAY: *Take a leisurely stroll and*
> *notice your surroundings.*

Go for a walk and shift your attention outward instead of inward. Notice your surroundings. Is the concrete wet or dry? Is the sky blue or gray? Do you see green leaves or red, orange, and brown ones?

Rather than walking to get from point A to point B, walk purely to notice and feel.

Write about your walk here. What did you notice on your journey?
How did you feel during and after your walk?

_____

_____

_____

_____

_____

_____

_____

_____

_____

_____

_____

_____

_____

_____

_____

_____

_____

_____

_____

_____

_____

_____

_____

Be Awed by the Human Spirit

At the 1992 Olympic Games, Derek Redmond was competing in the 400-meter semifinals when he tore his hamstring and collapsed.

To the crowd's shock, Derek got up and began hopping toward the finish line on one leg. He was determined to finish despite having no chance of winning. Derek's father, Jim, dashed over and looped Derek's arm over his shoulder for support, and together they made their way across the finish line.

When I saw a video of this, tears poured down my face. I was awestruck by the power of a father's love and reminded of how we can choose to go onward even when it's difficult.

TODAY: *Watch a video that reminds you of the strength of the human spirit.*

Watch the video I just mentioned, or watch a firefighter rescuing a family, a civil rights leader speaking up for justice, or anything that reminds you how strong humans can be.

Write about the video you watched. What was it about? How did it make you feel?

Explore Questions with No Answers

Some questions can be answered with a simple "yes" or "no." Some have no clear-cut answers.

TODAY: *Spend time exploring questions that we don't know the answers to.*

What is the point of life?

What happens before we are born?

What happens after we die?

What is time?

What existed before time as we know it?

What is waiting at the edge of our galaxy, beyond where any spaceships have traveled?

Allow your mind to float freely from question to question. The goal is not to find The Answer. The goal is simply to feel whatever emotions arise as you consider these unknowables. Maybe fear. Maybe curiosity. Maybe awe.

Write about one question that you explored. What was it? How did you feel as you considered it?

Experience Birth

There are few experiences more awe-inspiring than birth.

TODAY: *Have an experience with birth—
in some form or another.*

Watch birth videos online. Listen to podcasts where parents share their labor and delivery stories. Ask your mom, your grandma, or a close friend to describe her birth experience to you. Ask:

"What did it feel like to give birth?"

*"What do you remember most strongly
about that day?"*

*"Did you feel like a different person after going
through that experience? How so?"*

Write about what you encountered. How did you experience birth today? How did it make you feel?

_____

_____

_____

_____

_____

_____

_____

_____

_____

_____

_____

_____

_____

_____

_____

_____

_____

_____

_____

_____

_____

_____

_____

Experience
Death

My friend Susan sat with her father-in-law during the final moments of his life. He expressed one of his greatest regrets—that he never visited Paris. "And now," he said, "it's too late."

This experience lodged itself in Susan's heart. Shortly after, she took her daughter to Paris, where they visited galleries, walked arm-in-arm down cobblestone streets, and drank steaming cups of chocolat chaud. Susan vowed, "I will be the woman who dies filled with stories—not filled with regrets."

Experiencing death can remind us how we truly want to live.

> TODAY: *Have an experience with death—*
> *in some form or another.*

Study a decaying leaf on the ground. Volunteer at a hospice. Walk through a cemetery. Flip through photos of a loved one who has passed away. Read books about death, such as *When Breath Becomes Air* by Paul Kalanithi, *The Bright Hour* by Nina Riggs, or *The Top Five Regrets of the Dying* by Bronnie Ware. Or, watch a movie where death is central to the plot line such as *Soul* or *A Walk to Remember*.

How did you experience death today? Write about how this made you feel.

Witness
Incredible Artistry

Once, I attended a classical music performance. The musicians were high school students who were exceptionally talented and disciplined—part of an elite music academy. They played a piece by Vivaldi and the soaring notes brought me to tears.

I felt a strange rumble of emotions: awe, inspiration, even a twinge of jealousy. I recall thinking, "I hope that I can one day create something one-tenth as beautiful as what I just experienced."

> TODAY: *Witness a talented artist—dancer, musician, sculptor, painter—doing what they do best.*

Attend a live performance or watch a video. Allow yourself to be humbled and amazed by the miraculous things that human beings can do.

Write about the artistry that you witnessed. How did it make you feel?

Listen for Three Sounds

Your ears contain the smallest bones in your entire body, yet they allow you to hear the big, vast world around you. Your ears never rest, processing sound even when you are asleep. Take a moment of gratitude and wonder for what the human body can do.

TODAY: *Try a listening exercise where you identify three sounds.*

Sit or lie down comfortably. Close your eyes. Listen for three sounds.

1. Find a sound that is very far away—like the roar of a distant highway.

2. Find a sound that is very close—like the ticking of a clock on your wall.

3. Find a sound coming from your own body—like the sound of your breath.

Keep your eyes closed for a few minutes. Breathe. Notice the emotions and sensations that arise.

What was the first sound you listened to? The second? The third? Write about what you felt and sensed during this listening exercise.

_____

_____

_____

_____

_____

_____

_____

_____

_____

_____

_____

_____

_____

_____

_____

_____

_____

_____

_____

_____

_____

Take a Break from Social Media

Have you ever promised yourself you'd peek at "one thing real quick" on social media—and before you knew it, you'd spent three hours scrolling mindlessly? Each post blurred into the next and you could barely remember what you'd watched or read. When we rapidly consume content without any space to pause and reflect, we tend to feel exhaustion rather than awe.

TODAY: *Step away from social media for one day (or one week!).*

Instead of posting a photo of your meal, savor the meal. Instead of taking a selfie on a hiking trail, take a moment of quiet admiration and experience the vastness of the mountain.

Interrupt your usual patterns. Connect with something bigger than the pixels on your phone. See if this sparks a moment of awe.

Write about what you noticed when you took a break from social media.

Spend Time with an Animal

Spending time in nature can evoke feelings of awe. But if you don't have access to a waterfall or forest on this particular day, look for the nearest animal.

Animals remind us that we're not alone on this planet, that we coexist with millions of other species, and we are all connected. And, animals remind us to pause the hustle-bustle of our busy lives, slow down, and practice being rather than doing.

TODAY: *Spend some time interacting with an animal.*

Gaze into a dog's trusting eyes. Watch your cat leap nimbly from the counter to the floor. Look up and see a flock of birds moving across the sky in perfect V formation.

If you don't have access to a furry, feathery, or scaly creature today, choose an animal you love and research to learn more about them. Did you know that gorillas can learn sign language? Or that sharks existed in prehistoric times, around four hundred million years ago? Or that many birds choose one partner and mate for life? Learn an astonishing animal fact that rearranges your view of the world.

Write about your experience spending time with an animal. What animal causes you to feel awe? If you researched animals, what were you astonished to learn?

Wait
Differently

Waiting for food to arrive at a restaurant. Waiting for a meeting to begin. Waiting on the phone, on hold with your bank.

Waiting can feel boring. Not exactly an awe-inspiring experience. But what if it could be?

> TODAY: *The next time you're waiting,*
> *make a point to do it differently.*

Instead of glancing down at your phone to pass the time . . . don't. Look up. Take in your surroundings. See if you can find a tiny moment of awe. Notice a couple reuniting at the airport. Notice a squirrel leaping nimbly from one tree branch to another. Instead of waiting for something else to happen, notice what is happening right now.

What were you waiting for? What did you notice when you waited differently? How did you feel?

Explore an Unsolved Mystery

Do ghosts exist? Why do so many ships get lost in the Bermuda Triangle? Who built Stonehenge, and why? Is the so-called Planet X real, or just theoretical, and could it really be ten times bigger than Earth?

TODAY: *Investigate one of life's mysteries.*

Pick a question that you're curious about. Think about it. Research it. Talk about it with a friend. The deeper you dig, the more awe you may feel, as you realize there truly is no clear-cut answer.

Write about an unsolved mystery that fascinates you. What is it? When you think about it, what do you feel?

Watch a Magic Show

Once, I watched a world-renowned magician climb into a tank of water and hold his breath for seventeen minutes—something no human ought to be able to do. It was astonishing.

Was this an athlete showing what his body could do after years of training? An optical illusion? Real magic? To this day, I don't know. But I still remember the hush that fell across the audience, the murmured whispers in the crowd, the collective amazement we all felt.

> TODAY: *Watch a magician (in person or online)*
> *do a mind-blowing show.*

Notice the sensations that arise. Do you feel your heart racing? Do you burst into laughter? Get teary-eyed? What does magic feel like in your body?

What happened at the magic show you watched? How did you feel?

See the World from High Above

Have you heard of the overview effect? This is a cognitive shift reported by many astronauts.

When viewing planet Earth from outer space—a blue orb in vast black nothingness—many astronauts report intense emotions: awe, transcendence, and an increased sense of connection to all beings on Earth. Many return back home with a new perspective on life.

One NASA astronaut, Edgar Mitchell, described his experience as an "overwhelming sense of oneness and connectedness," an "explosion of awareness," and an "epiphany."

TODAY: *View Earth from outer space.*

Look at photos online, flip through a book or magazine, or watch a documentary about the cosmos. See if you notice the overview effect in your own mind and body.

When gazing at images or videos of Earth from space, what do you feel? Write about it here.

Surprise
Someone You Love

For Father's Day one year, I surprised my dad by flying home to visit. I rang the doorbell and when he opened it . . . he was stunned. He spluttered in confusion: "Huh? What? How?" It took him a moment to process what he was seeing! Then he pulled me into a hug. I could feel his joy wrapping all around me.

When you experience a moment that doesn't fit what you expect, it can spark intense emotions like astonishment, exhilaration, or even awe.

TODAY: *Do something unexpected for a loved one.*

This can be any surprise, big or small. Do something your loved one isn't anticipating. Create a moment of joy . . . for them. As emotion floods their body, share in that moment of connection. You're creating a meaningful memory together. They might be awestruck by your actions, and you may experience secondhand awe yourself.

Who did you surprise, and how did you surprise them? How did they feel? How did you feel?

Look for a Sign

Hawaiʻi Volcanoes National Park is one of my favorite places. While the name evokes bubbling lava, the park is usually quite peaceful. Tall trees. Cool temperatures. Wisps of steam. A hushed feeling, like the world is sleeping.

Once, when my friend Kanani was leading a few colleagues and me on a walk to the crater's rim, she couldn't decide which route to take us on. She told us, "Let's look for a sign."

A few moments later, we came across a red-and-white directional sign in the middle of the path. "Look," Kanani said with a chuckle. "It's a sign."

> TODAY: *Ask for a sign from the universe, God, or whatever term you prefer.*

Ask a question that's been on your mind, or ask for a sign regarding what to do next. Instead of trying to answer the question yourself, ask for direction from something bigger than you.

What is something you've been wondering about and would like to receive a sign about? If you found a sign, what was it? What does that sign mean to you?

Unplug for
One Day

New technological advancements may create awe for a short time, but the awe quickly fades. Something that seems miraculous (email, social media, or downloading a digital book in one-tenth of a second) soon becomes commonplace.

Does technology ruin our ability to feel awe? It depends on how you're using it. But one thing most of us can agree upon is that we use tech devices too much and would like to cut back.

> TODAY: *Take a screen-free day (no phone, tablet, computer, or television) and notice how it feels.*

What emotions do you notice? What sensations arise in your body? Does it feel easier to experience little moments of awareness or wonder when it's just you and the world . . . with no screen in between?

After unplugging for one day, what did you notice?

Read an Awe-Inspiring Story

You don't have to visit an incredible place—like the Grand Canyon—or witness an amazing, heroic act in person to feel awe. Just reading about it can prompt similar emotions.

TODAY: *Lose yourself in a story that inspires awe.*

Pick a short story, essay, or article. Or listen to a podcast or audiobook.

Read a hiker's description of their challenging 2,650-mile [4,265 km] journey along the Pacific Crest Trail. Read the true story of Daryl Davis, a Black musician who befriended two hundred members of the Ku Klux Klan, changed their hearts and minds, and inspired each of them to leave the KKK. Or read another story about a place (or person) that gives you goosebumps and takes your breath away.

What story did you read? While reading it, how did you feel?

Plan the Final 24 Hours of Your Life

If you knew that you had twenty-four hours to live, what would you do with your time?

TODAY: *Make a list of what your final day would include.*

Watch the sunrise. Savor the greatest meal of your life. Gather with people you love. Say the words you should have said years ago: "I love you." "I'm grateful." "All is forgiven."

Imagine a clock counting down from twenty-four hours to one. This may lead to a day of profound meaning. Or, at least, one of the most memorable days of your life.

If you had twenty-four hours to live, what would you do? EXTRA CREDIT: *Take your "final twenty-four" list and actually do it. Live one day as if it were your last.*

Eat with Awareness

Eating is ordinary. It's something many of us do three times a day, if not more, so it can feel mundane. But what if you disrupted your usual routine?

TODAY: *Eat your meals with a sense of awareness.*

Eat differently than you normally do. If you usually eat quickly, enjoy a leisurely meal. If you often eat at your desk, sit outside. Pattern disruption can spark awe.

As you eat, consider all the different interconnected miracles that happened—the farmer who planted the rice, the delivery driver who brought it to your local store, the chef who prepared it—just to create the meal in front of you.

What did you eat? While eating, what did you notice?

Sleep with Awe

It's difficult to feel awe when your mind is crowded with noisy thoughts. You could sail beneath a double rainbow while dolphins leap all around (or another equally awe-inspiring experience!) but if you're distracted by a barrage of thoughts about meetings, emails, or taxes, you're unlikely to experience awe. Your head is too full. There's no space for wonder.

Meditation reduces the chatter in our minds, making it easier to access emotions like gratitude, reverence, and transcendence.

Go online and search for "awe meditation." You'll find more than five million results. One I especially enjoy is called "Living in Awe" recorded by Annie Aitken, whose voice is supremely relaxing. Pick an awe meditation and play it before bedtime.

TODAY: *Let an awe meditation guide you into sleep.*

After concluding your meditation, tuck yourself into bed. Fall asleep with awe lingering in your mind and body.

What awe meditation did you find? While listening and meditating, what did you experience? EXTRA CREDIT: *Notice how you feel the next morning. Same as usual? Different? More refreshed?*

_____

_____

_____

_____

_____

_____

_____

_____

_____

_____

_____

_____

_____

_____

_____

_____

_____

_____

_____

_____

_____

_____

_____

Wake with Awe

Most people reach for their phone first thing in the morning. We immediately check social media, email, news, and texts, and begin the day feeling mentally cluttered and exhausted. It's a habit that's not exactly awe-inspiring.

TODAY: *Start your day with a moment of peace.*

Rather than immediately reaching for your phone, disrupt the pattern. Instead of looking at a digital screen, look at something different. Gaze out the window and notice the texture of the clouds. Cuddle up to your partner, dog, or cat. Listen to an awe-inspiring piece of music.

Write about what happened when you started your day with a moment of awe. EXTRA CREDIT: *Try doing this several days in a row. When you begin your day with awe, does the rest of your day feel different?*

Think about Loss

"I have some bad news . . ."

My friend explained that her husband—an energetic, gregarious man in his fifties who had seemed to be in perfect health—was battling cancer. I was stunned. It didn't seem possible that he could be sick.

That evening, I went home and looked at my own husband with different eyes. I imagined what it would be like to lose him. I wrapped my arms around him and said, "I love you," and squeezed tightly.

> TODAY: *Think about losing someone*
> *(or something) that you love.*

Take a full minute to really think about it, picture it, and feel it. Feel the emotions that arise, difficult as they may be. You may feel a bit frightened. You may feel humbled—small in the presence of immense powers that we can't control.

Who (or what) did you imagine losing? How did you feel? What did thinking about loss make you realize?

Look Back

Think back to one of the most powerful moments of awe you've ever experienced.

Were you hiking in the woods? Watching lightning crack across the sky? Or awestruck in the presence of tremendous compassion and generosity?

TODAY: *Relive a powerful moment of wonder.*

What was one of the most powerful moments of awe you ever experienced? Write down what you remember most strongly, what you saw or heard, and what you felt.

Look
Forward

Visualize yourself experiencing a future moment of awe.
My friend Susan calls this "pre-membering": remembering
something that hasn't happened yet, but likely will. Like a
premonition.

Your future wedding. Your future trip to the Great Barrier Reef.
Your future child on the day they are born.

> TODAY: *Imagine experiencing a moment of awe*
> *that's yet to happen.*

Choose a future experience. Write about it as if it's happening
right now. Use present-tense language. For instance, "I am
swimming in crystal-blue water . . ." rather than "One day I
will swim by the reef . . ."

See if you can experience flickers of awe, right now, before this
future event actually happens.

What future moment of awe are you experiencing right now? Write about it here, using the present tense.

Ask
for Help

Experiencing the goodness of the human spirit can spark awe.

When you have moments of realization like "People can be so incredibly kind," "I'm stunned by how generous my community is," or "I'm amazed by how many people want to help," it allows you to feel connected to a greater whole rather than isolated.

> TODAY: *Ask for help . . . and allow yourself to receive it.*

Perhaps you need help finishing a project, making a difficult decision, or staying motivated with a goal. Reach out to someone and ask for the help you need.

Asking for help requires being vulnerable and taking down your shield. Allow yourself to be deeply moved, even awestruck, by how people in your life show up for you.

What did you need help with? When you asked for help, what happened next?

Give Help

Research shows that feeling awe makes you more generous, altruistic, and likely to help others. Could the same be true in reverse?

TODAY: *Do something generous for somebody else (with no strings attached) and see what feelings it sparks.*

Help a friend apply for a job. Nominate a local business owner for an award. Buy coffee for the person in line behind you. Anonymously, and with no expectation of being repaid, send money to a friend who's struggling with medical bills. Or offer another act of generosity.

There's an expression that goes, "To make a friend, be a friend." Perhaps the same applies to awe. To feel wonder yourself, create a wonderful moment for someone else.

Write about who you helped today. How did it make you feel?

Have a Very Unusual Day

Each time you disrupt a predictable pattern, it's like opening a window in your brain. Awe can flood in.

TODAY: *Plan a day where everything is . . . different.*

Make it a complete departure from your usual routine. Take a day off from work, school, or whatever you normally do. Take a class on a topic you know nothing about. Walk backward. Eat breakfast for dinner.

If possible, do something to connect with a greater cause, like volunteering. Or do something that makes you feel small, like riding an elevator to the top of a building and gazing at the city skyline—all the interconnected streets, bridges, cars, and people.

What did you do on your very unusual day? How did you feel?

Gaze through a Microscope

Did you know that there are one hundred trillion cells in your body? Cells grow, serve their purpose, and die, and new cells are generated. Certain cells have a lifespan of seventy years while others exist for just three days. Every day, your body replaces billions of cells. You're becoming a new version of "you" all the time.

> **TODAY:** *Look at something incredibly tiny (such as cells dividing) through a microscope.*

If you don't have access to a microscope, watch a video online.

Think about the magnificent things that happen all the time, too small for our eyes to detect. Enormous miracles in a tiny speck.

What is the incredibly small thing you looked at today? What did you observe? How did you feel?

Experience
Something Ancient

When you're in the presence of something ancient, it reminds you how vast time is, and how small and fleeting each human life is in comparison.

TODAY: *Go experience something immensely old.*

A vase from five thousand years ago. A building that was constructed before you, your parents, and your grandparents were born. A mountain that took ten million years to form. A tree that has survived two world wars and is still standing. A song written before audio recording equipment existed.

Write about the ancient thing you experienced today. What was it?
How did it make you feel?

Experience Something New

My husband, Zach, was born with a disability. One leg is shorter than the other, and one of his feet does not bend at the ankle. Throughout his life, he has dealt with frequent pain, but he accepted "this is how it is" and always tried to make the best of it.

Then we learned about a new prosthetic device that could help. We got him fitted and he trained with physical therapists to learn how to use it. One week later, I watched Zach *run* across the room—without pain. I'd never seen my husband run. *Ever*. I burst into tears and felt awed by this new miracle device. It changed both of our lives.

TODAY: *Go experience something completely new.*

Do something you've never done before. Or learn about something new that just recently came into the world. Be awed by a new medical advancement, a new music album, or anything new that stirs emotion in you.

What is the new thing you experienced? How did you feel during this experience?

Be a Little Scared

A few days after I moved to Hawai'i, a hurricane hit the islands. My landlord boarded up the windows and asked if I had water, food, and a flashlight. Having grown up in Los Angeles, a city that gets very little rain, I had no clue what to expect.

As the storm descended, I was awestruck . . . and frightened. A staggering amount of water pounded the coast. Fortunately, the hurricane passed quickly and nobody was injured, although there was plenty of damage to roads and buildings.

When you feel afraid, you're right at the edge of awe. Humbled by enormous powers. Grateful to simply be alive.

TODAY: *Allow yourself to be just a little bit scared.*

Watch a video of a tsunami. Listen to thunder. Read about a historic earthquake. Experience something (safely) that makes you feel humility and tingles of fear. You don't have to (and please don't!) literally put yourself in danger to feel powerful emotions.

How did you let yourself be a little scared? What did you experience?
Write about how it made you feel.

Listen to Someone Describe Awe

Hearing someone describe awe can spark similar feelings in your own mind and body.

TODAY: *Ask someone to describe a moment when they felt awe.*

This might be an exquisitely beautiful performance, an experience in the wilderness, encountering birth or death, or something else.

Listen to their story. Ask:

"What were you doing?"

"What happened?"

"How did you feel?"

"Did you have a different perspective on life after this experience?"

"What shifted for you?"

Reflect on what happened when you asked someone to describe a moment of awe. What did they tell you? How did hearing their story make you feel?

Be Moved by a Powerful Speech

One of my favorite speeches is Fred Rogers (host of *Mister Rogers' Neighborhood*) speaking to the US Senate Subcommittee on Communications in 1969. In this speech, Rogers urges the Senate not to cut funding for public broadcasting. He explains why it's important to produce children's shows that teach compassion. We need shows that teach kids empathy, kindness, and how to manage emotions in healthy ways, rather than violent cartoons with characters fighting one another. The subcommittee chairman, initially cynical, melts under the power of Rogers's words. As the speech ends, the chairman is impressed and agrees to provide twenty million dollars for public television.

TODAY: *Listen to someone give a powerful speech.*

Search online for videos of "awe-inspiring speeches" and watch one. Be awed by the beauty of the human spirit and the good that people can do. Words can change hearts and minds—and even change the world.

Write about the speech you listened to. What was it about? How did hearing those words make you feel?

_____

_____

_____

_____

_____

_____

_____

_____

_____

_____

_____

_____

_____

_____

_____

_____

_____

_____

_____

_____

_____

_____

_____

Focus on the Good

Dacher Keltner, one of the world's leading researchers on awe, says that simply witnessing others doing good things can spark awe.

TODAY: *Focus on all the good that is present in our world.*

Read a story about a selfless act. Listen to a podcast about a courageous deed. Move through your day and look for something tender and pure. Perhaps you'll notice a child comforting their friend, or someone assisting a stranger as they board a bus.

Terrible things happen every day. Good things happen too. We can acknowledge the horrors in our world and fight to correct them—while simultaneously acknowledging the goodness that is present. We can hold these contradictions in our hearts at the same time.

What is something good you noticed today? What happened? Write about how you felt when you saw it.

Find Awe in an Unexpected Place

A professor of psychology visited inmates at a prison and talked to them about awe. Some mentioned feeling it from the sensation of sunlight on their skin, or while immersed in a sport. Even in the worst conditions imaginable, and even in the most unexpected places, we have the capacity to feel awe.

TODAY: *Seek out awe in an unlikely location.*

Go somewhere that feels ugly, harsh, or uninspiring to you. A trash dump. Concrete parking lot. Hectic suburban mall. Search for something small—light filtering through a window, a song that sparks emotion, a tiny moment of connection.

Can you find awe even where you least expect it?

What is the unexpected place where you found awe? What did you experience?

Say "Surprise Me"

When you experience something new and novel—something that disrupts what you expect—you're more likely to experience awe.

TODAY: *Be surprised.*

Go to a bar, and instead of ordering your usual beverage, tell the bartender, "Surprise me." Or let a friend plan a day of activities and tell them, "I don't want to know anything in advance. I'd like to be surprised."

Another option: Do something ordinary (attend a meeting, send an email, make dinner) but put yourself into a different mindset. Rather than assuming you know exactly how it's all going to play out, tell yourself, "I'm open to being surprised."

Journal about a surprise you experienced today. What happened? How did it make you feel?

Watch a
Master at Work

While visiting Japan, I was awestruck watching a chef meticulously peel a piece of ginger. She worked so nimbly and quickly, removing every knob and bit of skin, until the ginger was smooth like a polished stone. She had the level of mastery that comes from doing something ten thousand times. All I could think was, "Oh . . . *wow*."

TODAY: *Watch an expert at work in their field.*

In person or online, witness the work of a master chef, artisan, musician, or anyone who has attained excellence in their field.

Whose expertise did you observe today? What did they do? How did seeing this make you feel?

Travel . . . Anywhere

Traveling—even if you remain close to home—is one of the most powerful ways to spark awe.

TODAY: *Take a trip somewhere.*

Travel to an area of your neighborhood that you haven't visited before. Travel ten, twenty, or a hundred miles away. Travel across the world. Travel anywhere.

There will always be a million reasons to stay home. There's too much work to do. It's not the right time. Maybe next year. Set minor objections aside and take the trip anyway, because the benefits of travel outweigh the inconveniences.

What is the trip you have always longed to take?

What if you just . . . did it?

Write about where you traveled. What did you notice on this trip?
How did you feel?

Learn How Something Gets Made

As a child, one of my most prized possessions was a book that described how things got made. One page described how matchsticks were produced; another page, airplanes; and another, Girl Scout Cookies. I reread this book countless times, mesmerized by the descriptions and photos. (I was particularly entranced by the cookies!)

TODAY: *Discover how something comes into being.*

A car engine. A tube of toothpaste. A song. Marvel at all the interconnected pieces that come together to make it possible.

Wandering through a gas-station convenience store can spark awe when you consider all the billions of steps that occurred to fill shelves with each item.

What did you study being made? What makes it an awe-inspiring process?

Read a Story about Profound Transformation

My friend Nicole struggled with alcohol use disorder. One night, after binge drinking with friends from college, she boarded a train and became unconscious. She awoke at an unfamiliar train stop, with no idea how she got there, bleeding from a cut that she didn't remember getting. At the time, she laughed it off as just another wild night out on the town. However, as the years went on, she realized that she didn't want to live this way anymore. She wanted to change.

Recently, she celebrated twelve years of sobriety.

Nicole's story reminds me that no matter how bleak things become, change is always possible. Human beings have an astounding ability to transform. We are never too old. It is never too late.

> TODAY: *Read about someone's personal experience with profound transformation.*

It could be a story about recovery from a substance use disorder, like the one I just shared. Or it could be another kind of story that inspires you.

The human heart is mysterious. Miracles happen. Anything is possible.

What story about transformation did you read? Write about how you felt while reading it.

Challenge an Assumption

We all have assumptions that shape our view of the world. Assumptions we inherited from our families, from society, or from past experiences.

You might assume "being self-employed is risky and failure is likely," "marriage is hard work," "it's difficult to make more money," or "dogs can't communicate using words."

TODAY: *Question something you assume to be true.*

Choose something that seems like an ironclad fact. Find evidence (even just one example) to prove that the opposite may be true. Be open to the possibility that you might be wrong—or, at least, that things may be more nuanced than you thought.

When your understanding of the world is rattled, it's like a tiny earthquake in your mind. These little quakes can produce awe.

What is the assumption you chose to question? When you challenged it, what did you discover?

_____

_____

_____

_____

_____

_____

_____

_____

_____

_____

_____

_____

_____

_____

_____

_____

_____

_____

_____

_____

_____

_____

_____

Be Awestruck . . . Together

Experiencing awe makes us feel more connected to others. However, some researchers believe the reverse is true as well. Experiencing connection can spark awe.

> TODAY: *Share an awe-inspiring experience with one person (partner, family member, or friend) or with a crowd. Experience the power of togetherness.*

Hold hands with someone you love as you enjoy a breathtaking view together. Psychologist Jessica Koehler says that couples who experience awe together feel more "us-ness" and stronger feelings of intimacy and trust.

Or attend a sporting event and cheer along with the crowd. Go to a concert and feel the rhythm of hundreds of people clapping to the beat. Watch fireworks and gasp along with everyone surrounding you—hearts beating as one.

What kind of moment did you share with another person—or people?
What happened? What do you remember about this experience?

Say "Thank You" to Someone Who Awed You

Think of someone who has awed you. This person might be a leader who did something heroic. A family member who wowed you with their generosity. An artist who created something so beautiful, it took your breath away. It could be someone living or dead.

> TODAY: *Write a thank-you note to someone who has brought awe into your life.*

You can deliver this note to them or not.

Expressing your thanks can help you relive this moment of awe . . . all over again.

Write a thank-you note describing how you felt awe because of this person and expressing gratitude for this experience.

Experience
Awe Three Ways

Awe is not one-size-fits-all. An experience that sparks profound awe for one person may not create awe for another. You might feel awe staring into the starry sky on a camping trip, while your friend might feel awe looking at cells dividing under a microscope.

What if you tried out someone else's recipe for awe? Take a new approach.

TODAY: *Seek out three suggestions
for how to experience awe.*

Ask three people, "When do you feel awe?" Write down what they say.

Challenge yourself to do all three things today (or in the next week). A trio of awe!

See if their suggestions evoke awe in you, too. If so, incredible. If not, you'll still have a memorable time.

Who did you ask about awe? What did they tell you? Write about your experiences when you followed their suggestions. How did these experiences make you feel?

Find the Common Thread

I came across an article that explains how people from different cultures express laughter in text messages.

In the United States, we type LOL, which means "laughing out loud." In France, texters say MDR, which stands for "mort de rire," meaning "dying of laughter." In Sweden, ASG is short for "asgarv," meaning "to laugh intensely." In Thailand, the number five sounds like "ha," so texting 555 means "hahaha."

Despite our differences, we share so much in common.

TODAY: *Search for one common thread*
that all human beings share.

Find an example of how we are connected, not separate.

We all sing lullabies to our children. We all want shelter and warmth. We all laugh in text messages. By finding a common thread, you may feel an emotional shift from "me" to "we."

What is one thing we all have in common? Does this make you feel strongly connected to other human beings?

_____

_____

_____

_____

_____

_____

_____

_____

_____

_____

_____

_____

_____

_____

_____

_____

_____

_____

_____

_____

_____

_____

_____

Reflect on Your Year of Awe

You've spent fifty-two weeks seeking awe, feeling it, recording it. You've experienced a year of awe.

> **TODAY:** *Reflect on what you've experienced in the last year and how it has changed you.*

First, write your top Awe Experiences from the last year. When did you feel awestruck? Make a list of three experiences that stand out.

Second, reflect on what has changed for you. After a year of awe, do you feel different? More connected to others? Do you have a new perspective on life, death, or what it means to be human? Has it become easier to experience awe in small, everyday moments now that you've practiced quite a bit?

What are your top three awe experiences? Reflect on what has shifted for you during your year of awe. EXTRA CREDIT: *Discuss your realizations with someone you love. Tell them about your journey. And perhaps you'd like to begin a brand-new year of awe . . . and do 52 experiments all over again.*

_____

_____

_____

_____

_____

_____

_____

_____

_____

_____

_____

_____

_____

_____

_____

_____

_____

_____

_____

_____

_____

_____

Conclusion

CLOSING THOUGHTS

While writing this journal, I was in my third trimester
of pregnancy, purchasing a new home, and working
full-time and then some—squirreling away extra cash
in preparation for maternity leave.

As a small-business owner and the primary breadwinner
of my household, there was a large amount of responsi-
bility on my shoulders. It was an exciting time. And, if I'm
being honest, there were stressful moments too.

The day before I delivered the manuscript for *Awestruck*
to my publisher, I had a meltdown. Not a cute one.
An ugly-cry, puffy-face, full-on tantrum.

I sat on the floor of my closet, half-dressed, enormous
belly bulging out. I began sobbing because (a) none
of my clothes fit, (b) I had too many deadlines at work,
(c) there was never enough time to get everything done,
(d) the baby might arrive at any moment and I did
not feel ready, (e) our new fence (to keep wild pigs out
of our yard!) was apparently going to cost thousands
of dollars, and (f) I kept peeing on myself every time
I sneezed.

As woe-is-me tears gushed down my face, my dog, Zuki,
came trotting into my closet of doom. He licked my
hands and gazed at me comfortingly. I looked into his
eyes and felt awed. How amazing that this creature

could provide unconditional love and care, exactly when I needed it most. How did he know?

I picked myself off the floor of the closet (with considerable effort and a few grunts, I might add) and I vowed, "Today, I will find little moments of awe." I needed a mental shift and was determined to get it.

I walked to my office and tried to observe my surroundings with fresh eyes, as if walking down the road for the very first time. I listened to piano music that stirred deep emotion. I had lunch with a friend instead of sitting alone at my desk. We talked about her recent breakup, and I felt humbled by her resilience and courage.

Tiny moments of mindfulness, admiration, reflection, and awe . . . all throughout the day. Each one cleared distress and debris from my spirit like cleansing rain. A few hours after my meltdown, I felt noticeably different. Awe turned my whole day around.

Awe is a powerful medicine. It helps us handle stress better. It allows us to rise above trivial matters and connect with something bigger. It reminds us how interconnected we all are—how we are loved, surrounded, and supported by so many people, animals, and even unseen forces that can't be rationally explained. I am a better wife, sister, daughter, and friend after being awestruck. I suspect the same is true for you.

I hope this journal inspires you to seek awe in your every-day life. We all need to experience this miraculous emotion more often. Can you imagine how society would shift if every human being took a five-minute awe-break each day?

May we all find a bit of space in our lives for awe to flow in.

—Alex

Resources

FURTHER READING

Curious to learn even more about awe? These resources are an excellent place to start.

Allen, Summer. "Eight Reasons Why Awe Makes Your Life Better." *Greater Good* magazine, UC Berkeley, February 12, 2015. https://greater good.berkeley.edu/article/item/eight_reasons_why_awe_makes_your _life_better.

Allen, Summer. "The Science of Awe." White paper, John Templeton Foundation at the Greater Good Science Center, UC Berkeley, Berkeley, CA, September 2018. https://ggsc.berkeley.edu/images/uploads/GGSC -JTF_White_Paper-Awe_FINAL.pdf.

Anderson, Craig L., et al. "Are Awe-Prone People More Curious? The Relationship between Dispositional Awe, Curiosity, and Academic Outcomes." *Journal of Personality* 88, no. 4 (2020): 762–79.

Bernstein, Elizabeth. "Awe Makes You Feel Better. Here's a Surprising Way to Find It." *Wall Street Journal*, September 26, 2021. https://www .wsj.com/articles/awe-makes-you-feel-better-heres-a-surprising-way -to-find-it-11632664802.

DiGiulio, Sarah. "Why Scientists Say Experiencing Awe Can Help You Live Your Best Life." Better, NBC News, February 19, 2019. https://www .nbcnews.com/better/lifestyle/why-scientists-say-experiencing-awe -can-help-you-live-your-ncna961826.

Pearsall, Paul. *Awe: The Delights and Dangers of Our Eleventh Emotion*. Deerfield Beach, FL: Health Communications, 2007.

Pollan, Michael. *How to Change Your Mind: What the New Science of Psychedelics Teaches Us About Consciousness, Dying, Addiction, Depression, and Transcendence*. New York: Penguin Press, 2018.

Sima, Richard. "Why It Is Awesome That Your Brain Can Experience Awe." *Washington Post*, September 15, 2022. https://www.washington post.com/wellness/2022/09/15/awe-mental-health/.

Zhang, Jia Wie, et al. "Awe Is Associated with Creative Personality, Convergent Creativity, and Everyday Creativity." *Psychology of Aesthetics, Creativity, and the Arts*, October 7, 2021. https://doi .org/10.1037/aca0000442.

BIBLIOGRAPHY

Introduction

Page 8: Two researchers: Keltner, Dacher, and Jonathan Haidt. "Approaching Awe, a Moral, Spiritual, and Aesthetic Emotion." *Cognition and Emotion* 17, no. 2 (2003): 297–314.

Page 12: Says Newberg, when you experience: Rosenfeld, Jordan. "Scientists Are Trying to Solve the Mystery of Awe." The Cut, May 26, 2016. https://www.thecut.com/2016/05/scientists-are-trying-to -solve-the-mystery-of-awe.html.

Page 12: The parietal lobe controls: SpinalCord.com Team. "Parietal Lobe: Function, Location and Structure." SpinalCord.com, December 3, 2020. https://www.spinalcord.com/parietal-lobe.

Page 12: "A loss of the boundary": Andrew Newberg, quoted in Rosenfeld, "Scientists Are Trying to Solve the Mystery of Awe."

Page 13: the "isolated self": Keltner, Dacher. "Why Awe Is Such an Important Emotion." The Art & Science of Awe conference, Zellerbach Playhouse, UC Berkeley, June 4, 2016. Video, 29:41. https://greatergood .berkeley.edu/video/item/why_awe_such_important_emotion.

Page 14: One study found: Anwar, Yasmin. "Can Awe Boost Health?" *Greater Good* magazine, UC Berkeley, February 12, 2015. https://greater good.berkeley.edu/article/item/awe_boosts_health.

Page 14: Researchers took military veterans: Anwar, Yasmin. "Nature Is Proving to Be Awesome Medicine for PTSD." *Berkeley News*, UC Berkeley, July 12, 2018. https://news.berkeley.edu/2018/07/12/awe -nature-ptsd.

Page 14: In a study of four hundred high school students: Farmer Kris, Deborah. "Awe Might Be Our Most Undervalued Emotion. Here's How to Help Children Find It." *Washington Post*, November 30, 2021. https://www.washingtonpost.com/lifestyle/on-parenting/children -awe-emotion/2021/11/29/0f78a4b0-4c8e-11ec-b0b0-766bbbe79347 _story.html.

Page 15: In another study: Piff, Paul K., et al. "Awe, the Small Self, and Prosocial Behavior." *Journal of Personality and Social Psychology* 108, no. 6 (2015): 883–99.

Page 15: After experiencing awe: Rudd, Melanie, Kathleen D. Vohs, and Jennifer Aaker. "Awe Expands People's Perception of Time, Alters Decision Making, and Enhances Well-Being." *Psychological Science* 23, no. 10 (2012): 1130–36.

Page 15: Researchers asked fifty-two people: Stillman, Jessica. "New Study: A 15-Minute 'Awe Walk' Kills Stress and Loneliness and Boosts Happiness." *Inc.*, October 26, 2020. https://www.inc.com /jessica-stillman/happiness-loneliness-study-awe-walk.html.

Page 16: Neuropsychologist Paul Pearsall: Pearsall, Paul. *Awe: The Delights and Dangers of Our Eleventh Emotion*. Deerfield Beach, FL: Health Communications, 2007.

Page 16: According to Penman: Penman, Danny. "Is Awe Our Most Underrated and Powerful Emotion?" *Psychology Today*, September 7, 2018. https://www.psychologytoday.com/us/blog/mindfulness-in -frantic-world/201809/is-awe-our-most-underrated-and-powerful -emotion.

Page 16: As professors Luke Fernandez and Susan J. Matt put it: Fernandez, Luke, and Susan J. Matt. "Has Technology Killed Our Capacity for Awe?" *Sojourners*, February 5, 2020. https://sojo.net /articles/has-technology-killed-our-capacity-awe.

Page 18: As Deborah Farmer Kris writes: Farmer Kris, "Awe Might Be Our Most Undervalued Emotion. Here's How to Help Children Find It."

A Year of Awe

Page 32: Professors Kiminobu Sugaya: Sugaya, Kiminobu, and Ayako Yonetani. "Your Brain on Music." *Pegasus*, University of Central Florida, Summer 2017. https://www.ucf.edu/pegasus/your-brain-on-music/.

Page 52: Your ears contain the smallest bones: Twinkl. "Smallest Bone in the Body." Accessed April 3, 2023. https://www.twinkl.com/teaching -wiki/smallest-bone-in-the-body.

Page 52: Your ears never rest: Polo Park Hearing Center. "What Happens To Our Hearing When We Sleep?" *Winnipeg Hearing* (blog). https://poloparkhearing.com/hearing-when-we-sleep/.

Page 56: Animals remind us: Otte/Nowatschin, Jan. "How Many Animals Are in the World." *Animals Around the Globe*, July 25, 2022. https://www.animalsaroundtheglobe.com/how-many-animals-are -in-the-world/.

Page 56: Did you know that gorillas: The Gorilla Foundation. "Sign Language." Koko.org. Accessed April 24, 2023. https://www.koko.org /about/programs/project-koko/interspecies-communication/sign -language/.

Page 56: Or that sharks existed in prehistoric times: Two Oceans Aquarium. "Evolution's Ultimate Predator: Here Are Our Top 10 Prehistoric Sharks," *Two Oceans Aquarium* (blog), October 14, 2020. https://www.aquarium.co.za/news/evolutions-ultimate-predator -here-are-our-top-10-prehistoric-sharks.

Page 56: Or that many birds: Michele Berger. "Till Death Do Them Part: 8 Birds That Mate for Life," Audubon, February 10, 2012. https:// www.audubon.org/news/till-death-do-them-part-8-birds-mate-life.

Page 62: Is the so-called Planet X real: NASA. "Hypothetical Planet X." Solar System Exploration. Updated December 19, 2019. https://solar system.nasa.gov/planets/hypothetical-planet-x/in-depth/.

Page 66: Have you heard of the overview effect?: Stepanova, Ekaterina R., Denise Quesnel, and Bernhard E. Riecke. "Space—A Virtual Frontier: How to Design and Evaluate a Virtual Reality Experience of the Overview Effect." *Frontiers in Digital Humanities* 6 (2019). DOI: 10.3389/fdigh.2019.00007.

Page 66: One NASA astronaut, Edgar Mitchell: Edgar Mitchell, quoted in Yaden, David Bryce, et al. "The Overview Effect: Awe and Self-Transcendent Experience in Space Flight." *Psychology of Consciousness: Theory, Research, and Practice* 3, no. 1 (2016) 1–11.

Page 74: Read the true story of Daryl Davis: Brown, Dwane. "How One Man Convinced 200 Ku Klux Klan Members to Give Up Their Robes." NPR, August 20, 2017. https://www.npr.org/2017/08/20 /544861933/how-one-man-convinced-200-ku-klux-klan-members -to-give-up-their-robes.

Page 82: One I especially enjoy: Aitken, Annie. "Living in Awe." InsightTimer. Accessed April 24, 2023. https://insighttimer.com /annieaitken/guided-meditations/living-in-awe.

Page 84: Most people reach for their phone: Wheelwright, Trevor. "2023 Cell Phone Usage Statistics: Mornings Are for Notifications" Reviews.org, January 24, 2022. https://www.reviews.org/mobile /cell-phone-addiction/.

Page 102: Did you know that there are one hundred trillion cells: Atkinson, Matt. "Mapping the 100 Trillion Cells That Make Up Your Body." *University of Florida News*, October 16, 2018. https://news.ufl.edu/articles/2018/10/mapping-the-100-trillion-cells-that-make-up-your-body.html.

Page 102: Certain cells have a lifespan: Opfer, Chris, and Allison Troutner. "Does Your Body Really Replace Itself Every Seven Years?" HowStuffWorks, June 6, 2014. https://science.howstuffworks.com/life/cellular-microscopic/does-body-really-replace-seven-years.htm.

Page 114: One of my favorite speeches: Rogers, Fred. "Testimony before the Senate Subcommittee on Communications." United States Capitol, Washington, DC, May 1, 1969. Video, 6:50. https://www.youtube.com/watch?v=fKy7IjRr0AA.

Page 118: Dacher Keltner: Reese, Hope. "How a Bit of Awe Can Improve Your Health." *New York Times*, January 3, 2022. https://www.nytimes.com/2023/01/03/well/live/awe-wonder-dacher-keltner.html.

Page 122: A professor of psychology: Morgan, Eleanor. "Oh Wow! How Getting More Awe Can Improve Your Life—and Even Make You a Nicer Person." *Guardian*, September 23, 2022. https://www.theguardian.com/lifeandstyle/2022/sep/23/how-getting-more-awe-can-improve-your-life-and-even-make-you-a-nicer-person.

Page 138: Psychologist Jessica Koehler: Koehler, Jessica. "How Cultivating Awe Enhances Fulfillment in Your Relationship." Psychology Today, March 30, 2023. https://www.psychologytoday.com/us/blog/beyond-school-walls/202303/how-cultivating-awe-enhances-fulfillment-in-your-relationship.

Page 150: In the United States: Stefanescu, Andreea. "How Different Cultures Laugh Online? Educate Your E-Laugh." *School of Manners* (blog), March 19, 2019. https://www.theschoolofmanners.com/blog/https/wwwtheschoolofmannerscom/blog-page-url/new-post-title.

Acknowledgments

This journal was born because of so many people working together.

I'm so grateful for . . .

Everyone at Chronicle Books, with extra-special thanks to Claire Gilhuly, Katie Van Amburg, and Jessica Ling who made thoughtful edits to make this journal better, and Wynne Au-Yeung for the gorgeous design.

Lindsey Smith, my literary agent, business partner, and longtime friend.

Friends who inspired several true stories in this journal: Robert Hartwell, Susan Hyatt, Nicole Antoinette, Kate Lyness, Kanani Aton, Molly Masaoka, and many more. All of you, in different ways, inspire me to live with greater appreciation and wonder.

All the brilliant psychologists and academic researchers—particularly Dacher Keltner—who study the health benefits of awe. Your work informed so much of this journal, especially the section on the science of awe.

Zach and Zuki, my two favorite boys.

Nora, even before you arrived in this world, you have filled me with overwhelming awe and shifted my perspective on life.

You, the person holding this journal. Thank you for plucking this off a shelf, or adding it to your cart, and for deciding, "I want to experience more awe." What a beautiful thing.

ALEXANDRA (ALEX) FRANZEN is the author of seven books. She's the cofounder of a bookstore called One Idea Books & Gifts and a company called Get It Done, and she has worked as a copywriter and editor for fifteen years. Alex lives with her husband and daughter in Hawai'i. She loves searching for awe in everyday life. Find Alex's newsletter, books, and more at www.alexandrafranzen.com.